IG 780L

Slight liquid damage 7/21 cc

Our National Parks

by Lucia Raatma

Content Adviser: Kathleen M. Kendrick, Project Historian,
National Museum of American History, Smithsonian Institution

Social Science Adviser: Professor Sherry L. Field,
Department of Curriculum and Instruction,
College of Education, The University of Texas at Austin

Reading Adviser: Dr. Linda D. Labbo, Department of Reading Education,
College of Education, The University of Georgia

Compass Point Books
Minneapolis, Minnesota

Compass Point Books
3722 West 50th Street, #115
Minneapolis, MN 55410

Visit Compass Point Books on the Internet at *www.compasspointbooks.com* or e-mail your
request to *custserv@compasspointbooks.com*

Photographs ©: PhotoDisc, cover; David Falconer, 4, 14; Jeff Greenberg/Visuals Unlimited, 6; Unicorn Stock
Photos/Jeff Greenberg, 8; Beth Davidow/Visuals Unlimited, 10; Spencer Swanger/Tom Stack & Associates, 12;
Photo Network/Jim Schwabel, 16; James P. Rowan, 18; Photo Network/Myrleen Cate, 20.

Editors: E. Russell Primm and Emily J. Dolbear
Photo Researchers: Svetlana Zhurkina and Jo Miller
Photo Selector: Linda S. Koutris
Designer: Melissa Voda

Library of Congress Cataloging-in-Publication Data
Raatma, Lucia.
    Our national parks / by Lucia Raatma.
        p. cm. — (Let's see library)
    Includes bibliographical references and index.
    ISBN 0-7565-0195-4
    1. National parks and reserves—United States—Juvenile literature. [1. National parks and reserves.]   I. Title.
II. Series.
    E160 .R33 2002
    973—dc21   2001004486

Table of Contents

What Is a National Park?

A national park is an area set aside by the government to protect land, plants, and animals. We create national parks so that certain areas will always remain the way they are today.

National parks were started in the late 1800s. The U.S. Congress decided to preserve parts of the country's land. Companies cannot build on this land. People cannot build houses here. No one is allowed to damage or remove anything in these areas, not even a flower. People all over the country enjoy nature in our national parks.

◄ *National parks protect animals, such as this antelope in Montana's Glacier National Park.*

Where Are Our National Parks?

Fifty-two national parks are located all over the United States. About half of the states have national parks.

The U.S. Virgin Islands have a national park, too. This **sanctuary** lies mainly on St. John Island. A sanctuary is a natural area where **wildlife** is protected from hunting. Virgin Islands National Park is home to sea turtles, large lizards called iguanas, and more than thirty kinds of tropical birds.

◀ *Virgin Islands National Park is in the Caribbean Sea.*

What Kinds of Parks Do We Have?

The United States has all kinds of national parks. Some parks are big canyons. The Grand Canyon is one of the best-known parks. Others have large forests and towering mountains.

Some parks are mostly desert areas. Parts of the Mojave and Colorado Deserts make up Joshua Tree National Park. Some parks, such as Crater Lake, consist mainly of lakes and rivers.

Acadia National Park in Bar Harbor, Maine, lies along the Atlantic Ocean. It has a beautiful lighthouse. The Hawaii Volcanoes National Park includes two active volcanoes!

◀ *Joshua Tree National Park in California has many cactus plants and colorful flowers.*

What Was the First National Park?

The first national park was Yellowstone National Park. It lies mostly in Wyoming, but it also spreads into Idaho and Montana. In 1872, it became the first park of its kind in the world.

Yellowstone is very big. It has 2,219,791 acres (899,015 hectares) of land. The park is larger than the states of Rhode Island and Delaware combined!

Millions of people come to Yellowstone each year. They may see elk, bison, bears, and many kinds of birds. The park is famous for a **geyser** called Old Faithful.

◄ Elk feed on grass below snowy hills in Yellowstone National Park.

What Problems Do National Parks Face?

Some people believe that national parks have too many visitors. Fishing and boating have hurt Florida's Biscayne and Dry Tortugas National Parks. Beachgoers have damaged some fragile **coral reefs**. In some parks, jet skis pollute the water and snowmobiles destroy wildlife.

Pollution in the air and soil is another problem for national parks. Companies dump chemicals that poison the soil near some parks. Those chemicals kill the plants—and the animals that eat those plants. Many national parks are in danger because of pollution.

◄ *These cross-country skiers enjoy Grand Teton National Park without harming the environment.*

Who Takes Care of Our National Parks?

The National Park Service takes care of all the U.S. parks. The National Park Service was created in 1916. This group has its main office in Washington, D.C. It also has ten offices in various parts of the country.

Each park has its own staff. The parks have **rangers** as well as scientists and tour guides. Visitors may also help take care of the parks. They can respect the plants and animals. They can carry out their trash and be sure to put out their fires.

◄ A park ranger in Grand Teton National Park shows off a raccoon that lives in the area.

How Do People Enjoy Our National Parks?

People enjoy our national parks in many ways. Some people camp in the parks. Others ride horseback, fish, or snorkel. At Carlsbad Caverns National Park in New Mexico, visitors may explore an exciting underground world.

Animal lovers may see deer, moose, bald eagles, sea lions, and many other kinds of animals in national parks. Visitors to Florida's Everglades National Park will see lots of alligators.

Some people hike, bike, swim, ski, or canoe through the parks on their own. Others prefer guided tours. Our national parks offer many activities.

◄ *Visitors to Everglades National Park in Florida might see giant alligators like this one.*

How Can You Visit Our National Parks?

Find out which national parks are near your home. Think about which parks might be fun to visit. Talk to your parents or teachers about planning a trip. Call or write for information about the national parks, or visit the Internet sites. Look for addresses and web sites on page 23. You'll find lots of interesting national parks to choose from.

◄ *Rocky Mountain National Park in Colorado is one of our most popular national parks.*

Why Are National Parks Important?

National parks keep natural areas from being destroyed. They provide homes for many kinds of animals. They protect the **endangered species** that live in the parks. Without our national parks, certain plants and animals could die out.

Many people enjoy spending time in natural spaces. National parks keep those areas safe. Both wildlife and people benefit from our national parks.

◀ *A man enjoys biking through Yosemite National Park in California.*

Glossary

coral reefs—colorful underwater structures made up of the skeletons of tiny sea creatures

endangered species—plants or animals that are at risk of dying out

geyser—a spring that produces jets of heated water and steam

rangers—people who guard parks and forests

sanctuary—a natural area where wildlife is protected

wildlife—plants and animals living in their natural environment

Did You Know?

• National parks are created by Congress and by the president of the United States.

• About 275 million people visit National Park Service sites each year. In 1998, the total number of people living in the United States was a little more than 270 million.

• Some national parks were bought by citizens and given to the country.

Want to Know More?

At the Library

Halvorsen, Lisa. *Letters Home from Yellowstone*. Woodbridge, Conn.: Blackbirch, 2000.

Meister, Cari. *Grand Canyon*. Edina, Minn.: Abdo and Daughters, 2000.

Weber, Michael. *Our National Parks*. Brookfield, Conn.: Millbrook Press, 1994.

On the Web

National Parks Conservation Association
http://www.npca.org/flash.html
For more information about protecting the national parks

Visit Your Parks
http://www.nps.gov/parks.html
For information about visiting the nation's parks

Through the Mail

National Park Service
1849 C Street, N.W.
Washington, DC 20240
To find out more about national parks

On the Road

Grand Canyon National Park
Grand Canyon, AZ 86023
520/638-7888
To visit one of the world's most beautiful places

Index

About the Author

Lucia Raatma received her bachelor's degree in English literature from the University of South Carolina and her master's degree in cinema studies from New York University. She has written a wide range of books for young people. When she is not researching or writing, she enjoys going to movies, playing tennis, practicing yoga, and spending time with her husband, daughter, and golden retriever. She lives in New York.